soups

igloo

igloo

Published by Igloo Books Ltd
Cottage Farm
Sywell
NN6 0BJ
www.igloo-books.com

10 9 8 7 6 5 4 3 2

ISBN: 978 1 84817 639 3

Project Managed by R&R Publications Marketing Pty Ltd

Food Photography: R&R Photostudio (www.rrphotostudio.com.au)
Recipe Development: R&R Test Kitchen

Front cover photograph © Stockfood/Antje Plewinski

Printed and manufactured in India

contents

introduction

All over the world, a bowl of soup speaks of love, warmth and comfort. Just a few spoonfuls fills us with a tangible serenity, as real as the fragrant liquid that nourishes our bodies and satisfies our soul.

Soup is one of our most basic foods. Its history stretches far into the past when soup was simply water simmered with whatever basic ingredients were available for flavour. Soup then was never about quality ingredients and complex flavours. Rather, it was simply about survival. Yet soup was still a meal shared between family members and acquaintances.

Thick hearty soups are served in the cold months to nourish and satisfy hungry children and to give energy to busy people at the end of a hectic day. Cold refreshing soups are served in hot and humid climates to invigorate and enliven after an exhausting hot day.

Throughout the Western world soups are served as a teaser to the coming meal, while in China soup is served after the meal as an invigorating finale. In many European countries soup is served between courses to refresh the palate.

In fact soup is served more often and in many more flavour combinations throughout the world than any other meal.

vegetable soups

Chilled Red Pepper and Fennel Soup

(see photograph on page 6)

2 tablespoons olive oil

2 leeks, white part only, chopped

1 onion, chopped

2 cloves garlic, chopped

2 shallots, chopped

5 large carrots, chopped

2 fennel bulbs, halved, cored and chopped

4 sprigs fresh thyme

2–3 red peppers

1 cup champagne or white wine

4½ cups vegetable stock

salt and freshly ground pepper

3 tablespoons mild yoghurt

MINTED CORN SALSA

2 ears of corn

½ small onion, finely diced

1 tomato, seeded

10 fresh mint leaves, finely sliced

2 sprigs fresh coriander, chopped

⅓ cup chopped fresh parsley

juice of 1 lime

salt and freshly ground pepper

1   Heat the olive oil in a saucepan and add the leeks, onion, garlic and shallots and sweat for 5 minutes until soft. Add the carrots, fennel and thyme sprigs and cook over a medium heat for 30 minutes until all the vegetables are tender.

2   Meanwhile, slice the four sides of the peppers (discard the seed core) and grill, skin side up, for about 5 minutes until blackened and blistered. Transfer the capsicums into a plastic bag and allow to steam. When cool enough to handle, open the bag and slip the skins off the pepper pieces. Add the capsicum pieces, champagne and stock to the softened vegetables and raise the heat to high.

3   Continue to cook, uncovered for 20 minutes until all the flavours have combined. Remove the soup from the heat and purée in a food processor, blender or with a hand blender. Season to taste with salt and pepper and allow to cool.

4   Make the salsa by cutting all the corn off the ears and microwaving on high for 2 minutes. Mix the onion, tomato and corn in the bowl. Add the mint leaves, coriander, parsley, lime juice and salt and pepper to taste and mix thoroughly. To serve, ladle the soup into individual bowls, top with some yoghurt and a generous spoonful of minted corn salsa.

5   This soup is delicious served with toasted Italian bread. To make, cut Italian bread into thick slices, place on a baking tray at 180°C for 10 minutes, turn bread and bake for 10 minutes longer or until golden. Rub hot toast with the cut surface of a clove of garlic. Serve immediately.

Serves 8

French Onion Soup

(see photograph opposite)

6 large onions, thinly sliced

3 cloves garlic, finely chopped

2 tablespoons olive oil

5 cups hot water

4 vegetable stock cubes

½ cup grated Gruyère cheese

6 x 1cm slices large diameter baguette

1   Heat the oil in a large saucepan and sauté the onions and garlic over a medium heat until onions are golden brown. Pour over hot water and crumble in stock cubes. Cover and cook for 20 minutes. While soup is cooking, sprinkle the cheese evenly over bread. Grill until golden. Serve soup topped with a grilled cheese crouton.

Serves 4–6

Minestrone

4¼ cups vegetable stock

440g can peeled tomatoes, chopped

2 cups dry white wine

2 onions, diced

3 carrots, diced

1 turnip, diced

2 sticks celery, sliced

2 red peppers, diced

1 large courgette, sliced

500g can red kidney beans, drained

¾ cup elbow macaroni or penne pasta

½ teaspoon ground turmeric

salt and pepper

PESTO

1 bunch fresh basil

3 cloves garlic, crushed

60g Parmesan cheese, finely grated

½ cup olive oil

salt and pepper

1 Place the stock, tomatoes, wine, onions, carrots, turnip, celery and peppers in a large saucepan. Bring to the boil, reduce the heat and simmer for 20 minutes.

2 Add the courgette, kidney beans, pasta and turmeric. Simmer for a further 40 minutes, stirring regularly, until the vegetables are tender. Season with salt and pepper. To make the pesto place the basil, garlic and Parmesan cheese in a food processor or blender. Blend until finely chopped. While the motor is running, gradually add the olive oil through the feed tube until a paste is formed.

3 Season with salt and pepper. Serve the soup in large soup bowls. Stir in 1 tablespoon of pesto into each bowl.

Serves 10

French Vegetable Soup with Pistou

460g fresh borlotti or dried navy beans

30g butter

1 large onion, finely chopped

460g green beans, trimmed

500g courgette or squash, cut into
  0.5cm-thick slices

6 medium potatoes, cut into 1cm cubes

3½ litres water

1–2 teaspoons salt (the amount of
  vegetables calls for a good seasoning)

60g farfalle (pasta bows)

PISTOU

1 cup fresh basil leaves

4 cloves garlic

1 large tomato

1 tablespoon tomato paste

½ cup grated Parmesan or Gruyère
  cheese

3 tablespoons olive oil

1 If using dried beans, soak overnight. Place the soaked and drained dried beans in a pan with fresh water to cover. Bring to the boil, cover and simmer gently for 15 minutes. Drain. Melt the butter in a large deep pan and sauté the vegetables, including the beans, until softened for about 5 minutes.

2 Cover with cold water and add salt. Cover and simmer gently for 1 hour. Add the farfalle to the soup, cooking for a further 15 minutes. Make pistou by processing the basil with the garlic in a food processor or blender. Peel and chop the tomato and add to the basil with the tomato paste and cheese.

3 Purée to a paste, adding oil gradually through the feed tube. Stir the pistou into the soup just before serving. Serve piping hot with crusty bread.

Serves 4–6

Fresh Spring Green Soup

8 dried shiitake mushrooms

8 cups light vegetable stock

6 cloves garlic, peeled

50g piece fresh ginger, sliced

1 bunch chard, washed and sliced

3 courgette, finely sliced

1 small head of broccoli, divided into tiny florets

200g peas, shelled

4 spring onions, sliced thinly diagonally

100g sugar snap peas

2 handfuls baby spinach

salt and freshly ground black pepper

1 Soak the shiitake mushrooms in a small bowl of hot water until soft, for about 20 minutes. Drain, discarding the water, and then slice the mushrooms into thin strips. Place the stock in a large saucepan with the garlic and ginger and bring to the boil. Simmer for 15 minutes.

2 Discard the garlic and ginger. Add the mushrooms, chard, courgette, broccoli and peas and simmer for 8–10 minutes. Add the spring onions, sugar snap peas and baby spinach and simmer for 2 minutes. Season to taste with salt and pepper then serve hot.

Serves 6

Carrot and Lentil Soup

30g butter

1 tablespoon sunflower oil

500g carrots, chopped

1 onion, chopped

2 sticks celery, chopped

125g red split lentils, rinsed

1 litre vegetable stock

salt and freshly ground black pepper

plain yoghurt and chopped fresh
  parsley to garnish

1 Melt the butter with the oil in a saucepan and fry the carrots, onion and celery for 6–8 minutes or until lightly golden. Add the lentils and 2 1/2 cups of the vegetable stock and bring to the boil. Cover and simmer for about 20 minutes, until the carrots are tender.

2 Allow the soup to cool for about 15 minutes, then purée in a blender or food processor until smooth. Return to a clean saucepan with the remaining stock, add seasoning to taste and reheat gently before serving. Add a swirl of yoghurt and a sprinkling of chopped fresh parsley to garnish.

Serves 4

Minestrone Piemonte

½ cup small white beans

½ cup kidney beans

½ cup chickpeas

4 white onions, chopped

2 cloves garlic, minced

3 tablespoons olive oil

½ small cabbage, sliced

2 sticks celery, sliced

2 medium carrots, sliced finely

6 cups good quality vegetable stock

2 tablespoons tomato paste

12 basil leaves, chopped

6 sprigs parsley

3 bay leaves (fresh if possible)

salt and pepper to taste

100g piece Parmesan rind

4 courgettes, sliced

1 cup good red wine

1   The night before, mix the white beans, kidney beans and chickpeas together and soak in cold water overnight. (If you don't have time to soak the beans overnight, cover them with hot water for 2 hours then drain and proceed with the recipe).

2   Sauté the onions and garlic in the olive oil for 5 minutes or until soft. Add the cabbage, celery and carrots and sauté for a further 5 minutes or until the vegetables have softened.

3   Add the beef stock, tomato paste, soaked bean mixture, basil, parsley, bay leaves and salt and pepper to taste and simmer for 2 hours or until thick and fragrant. Add the Parmesan cheese rind, sliced courgette, red wine and a little extra water if necessary to thin the soup. Cook for a further 30 minutes, remove bay leaves and serve.

Serves 4

Note: A particularly nice touch is to finish each bowl with a spoonful of pesto. The heat of the soup warms the pesto and allows it to permeate throughout the entire bowl of soup.

Porcini Mushroom Soup

1 tablespoon dried Porcini

½ cup boiling water

2 tablespoons olive oil

2 cloves garlic, minced

1 leek, cleaned and chopped

6 shallots, chopped

285g white mushrooms

500g forest mushrooms, including porcini, shiitake, oyster and swiss brown

2 tablespoons flour

4 cups good quality chicken, beef or vegetable stock

1 cup double cream

½ bunch flat-leaf parsley, chopped

30 basil leaves, sliced

1 tablespoon fresh oregano

salt, pepper and nutmeg, to taste

1 Add the dried Porcini to the boiling water and set aside. When the mushrooms have softened, remove them from the mushroom water and set aside. Strain the mushroom liquid through a paper towel or muslin-lined sieve to separate sand and grit, and reserve the liquid.

2 Heat the olive oil and add the garlic, leeks and shallots and cook until golden (about 3 minutes). Add all the fresh mushrooms, thinly sliced, and cook over a very high heat until the mushrooms soften and their liquid evaporates (about 6 minutes). Reserve a few mushroom pieces for a garnish.

3 Sprinkle with the flour and stir well to enable the flour to be absorbed. Add the chicken stock and the Porcini mushrooms together with the soaking liquid and bring to the boil, stirring frequently.

4 Once the soup is boiling, reduce the heat to a simmer and cook for 30 minutes. Add the cream and simmer for a further 5 minutes or until slightly thickened. Add half the chopped parsley, sliced basil and oregano and season to taste with salt and pepper.

5 To serve, ladle into individual bowls, sprinkle with extra parsley, reserved mushrooms, some nutmeg and a small dollop of extra cream if desired.

Serves 6

Note: To make a low-fat version of this delicious soup, substitute evaporated skim milk instead of the cream.

Chilli Kumara Soup

6 cups vegetable stock

3 stalks fresh lemongrass, bruised or
 1½ teaspoons dried lemongrass,
 soaked in hot water until soft

3 fresh red chillies, halved

10 slices fresh or bottled galangal or
 fresh ginger

5–6 fresh coriander plants, roots
 washed, leaves removed and reserved

1 large kumara (orange sweet potato),
 peeled and cut into 2cm pieces

¾ cup coconut cream

1 tablespoon Thai fish sauce (nam pla)

1 Place stock, lemongrass, chillies, galangal or ginger and coriander roots in
   a saucepan and bring to the boil over a medium heat. Add kumara (sweet
   potato) and simmer, uncovered, for 15 minutes or until kumara is soft.

2 Remove lemongrass, galangal or ginger and coriander roots and discard.
   Cool liquid slightly, then purée soup, in batches, in a food processor or
   blender. Return soup to a clean saucepan and stir in 125ml of the coconut
   cream and the fish sauce. Cook, stirring, over a medium heat for 4 minutes
   or until heated. Stir in ⅔ of the reserved coriander leaves.

3 To serve, ladle soup into bowls, top with a little of the remaining coconut
   cream and scatter with remaining coriander leaves.

Serves 4

Chickpea, Roasted Tomato and Garlic Soup

500g dried chickpeas

1 kg tomatoes

1 bulb garlic

75ml olive oil

salt

2 tablespoons dried oregano

2 leeks, sliced, white part only

4 cups vegetable stock

2 tablespoons tomato paste

salt and pepper

oregano leaves, fresh

1 Soak chickpeas in cold water overnight. Place chickpeas in a saucepan covered with water and bring to the boil, then simmer for approximately 1 hour until chickpeas are cooked. Drain and set aside.

2 Preheat the oven to 200°C. Halve the tomatoes and place them in a baking tray. Cut the top off the garlic bulb and place it in the baking tray.

3 Drizzle with olive oil, sprinkle with salt and dried oregano, and roast in the oven for 20–30 minutes.

4 Place the tomatoes and 5 peeled garlic cloves (reserve the rest) in a food processor, and purée for 1 minute.

5 Heat half the oil and sauté the leeks for 3 minutes. Add the stock, and bring to the boil, then reduce heat to simmer.

6 Add the tomato mixture, tomato paste and the chickpeas, season with salt and pepper, and heat through.

7 Sprinkle with fresh oregano leaves just before serving.

Serves 4

Pappa al Pomodoro

7 cups good quality vegetable stock

6 tablespoons olive oil

2 onions, peeled and roughly chopped

3 cloves garlic, minced

2 red peppers, finely chopped

1⅓ kg ripe tomatoes, preferably home–grown

2 tablespoons tomato paste

400g stale white bread

½ bunch fresh basil, roughly torn

salt and freshly ground pepper, to taste

1 Heat the stock in a saucepan and allow to simmer.

2 Heat the olive oil and add the onion, garlic and peppers and cook until softened. Add the roughly chopped tomatoes and tomato paste and cook over a medium heat for 10 minutes. Purée this mixture then return it to the saucepan.

3 Remove the crusts from the bread and discard them. Dice the bread into small cubes.

4 To the tomato mixture, add the stock, together with the bread, basil and salt and pepper to taste.

5 Cover and simmer for about 45 minutes, then stir vigorously with a wooden spoon to break up the bread cubes.

6 Serve either hot or at room temperature, with a few extra pieces of basil and some freshly ground black pepper.

Serves 4

Note: For a smoother texture, purée the soup briefly to break up some of the bread cubes, but be careful not to over-process the soup.

Yellow Pepper Soup with Red Pepper Harissa

2 teaspoons olive oil

3 yellow peppers, diced

1 carrot, finely diced

1 small onion, diced

1 cup potato, diced

2 cups hot vegetable stock

2 teaspoon orange zest, grated

juice of 1 orange

RED PEPPER HARISSA

2 red peppers, cut in half lengthwise, seeds removed

1 Roma tomato, cut in half lengthwise, seeds removed

1 tablespoon red wine vinegar

2 teaspoons no-added-salt tomato paste

hot chilli sauce

freshly ground black pepper, to taste

1 Heat the oil in a non-stick saucepan over a low heat. Add the yellow peppers, carrot and onion. Cook, stirring, for 10 minutes or until the peppers are soft. Add the potato and stock. Bring to simmering. Simmer for 20 minutes or until the potato is soft. Cool slightly.

2 Transfer mixture to a food processor. Add orange zest and juice. Purée. Season with black pepper to taste. Return soup to a clean saucepan. Reheat.

3 To serve, ladle soup into warm bowls. Top with harissa.

HARISSA

1 Preheat grill to hot. Using your hands, gently flatten the red pepper and tomato halves and place, skin side up, on aluminium foil under the grill. Cook until skins blacken. Set aside until cool enough to handle. Remove skins.

2 Place pepper and tomato flesh in a food processor. Add vinegar, tomato paste and hot chilli sauce and black pepper to taste. Purée. Set aside until ready to serve.

Serves 4

Borscht with Cucumber Yoghurt

1 tablespoon olive oil

1 onion, thinly sliced

1 clove garlic, crushed

1cm piece fresh ginger, grated

1 tablespoon tomato paste

3 large beets, thinly sliced

1 large potato, thinly sliced

1 parsnip, thinly sliced

1 bay leaf

6 cups vegetable stock

2 tablespoons red wine vinegar

juice of 1 lemon or orange

freshly ground black pepper

CUCUMBER YOGHURT

½ bunch fresh chives

¼ cup cucumber, finely diced

1 tablespoon fresh dill, chopped

1 teaspoon lemon juice

1 cup thick low-fat plain yoghurt

1 Heat the oil in a large, non-reactive saucepan over a medium heat. Add the onion, garlic and ginger. Cook, stirring, for 5 minutes or until ingredients are soft.

2 Stir in the tomato paste. Cook for 1–2 minutes. Add the beets, potato and parsnip. Cook, stirring, for 2–3 minutes. Add the bay leaf, stock, vinegar and lemon juice. Bring to the boil, then reduce heat. Cover. Simmer for 30–40 minutes or until vegetables are soft. Season with black pepper to taste. Cool slightly.

3 Transfer mixture to a food processor or blender, and purée in batches. Return the soup to a clean saucepan. Bring back to the boil. Check seasoning. Add more lemon juice if necessary.

4 To serve, ladle soup into warm bowls. Top with a spoonful of the cucumber yoghurt.

CUCUMBER YOGHURT

1 Bring a saucepan of water to the boil. Blanch the chives. Drain well. Place the chives in a food processor. Add the cucumber, dill and lemon juice, and process to make a paste. Transfer mixture to a bowl. Stir in yoghurt. Cover. Refrigerate until ready to use.

Serves 6

Sweet Potato, Pasta and Leek Soup

2 teaspoons rapeseed oil

2 leeks, thinly sliced

pinch saffron

1 kg sweet potato, peeled and chopped

8 cups vegetable stock

1 cinnamon stick

1 bouquet garni

125g ditalini (tiny pasta pieces for soup)

2 tablespoons fresh chives, chopped

LAVASH CRISPS

2 sheets lavash bread

1 tablespoon olive oil

2 tablespoons Parmesan cheese, finely grated

1 Heat the oil in a large pot, add the leeks and cook over a medium heat for 5 minutes or until the leeks are soft and golden. Add the saffron and sweet potato and stir for about 5 minutes or until the sweet potato begins to soften.

2 Stir in the stock, cinnamon stick and bouquet garni. Bring to the boil then reduce the heat and simmer for 30 minutes, or until the sweet potato is very soft. Remove the cinnamon stick and bouquet garni.

3 Cook the pasta in a large pot of rapidly boiling water until al dente (cooked, but still with a bite to it). Drain well.

4 Purée the soup in batches until smooth, then return to the pot along with the pasta and reheat gently. If it is too thick add a little water.

LAVASH CRISPS

1 Use a star-shaped cookie cutter to cut out shapes from the bread, brush lightly with oil, sprinkle with parmesan cheese and place another star on top. Grill until crisp and golden.

2 To serve, ladle the soup into bowls, float lavash stars on top and sprinkle with chives.

Serves 6

Spinach and Nutmeg Soup with Cheese Toasts

2 tablespoons olive oil

30g butter

250g floury potatoes, peeled and cut into 2½cm cubes

250g spinach leaves

1 teaspoon nutmeg, freshly grated

6 cups vegetable stock

salt and black pepper

CHEESE TOASTS

4 tablespoons crème fraîche

100g Gruyère, Caerphilly or Cheddar cheese, grated

1 large egg, beaten

day-old narrow French bread stick, cut diagonally into 18 x 1cm slices

1 Heat the oil and half the butter in a large saucepan. Fry the potatoes for 1 minute, then add the spinach and the nutmeg. Cook for 2 minutes or until the spinach is wilting.

2 Add the stock to the potato and spinach mixture, season lightly and bring to the boil. Reduce the heat, cover and simmer for 10–15 minutes, until the potatoes are tender. Leave to cool for 10 minutes.

3 Pour the soup into a food processor and blend until smooth, or use a hand blender. Stir in half the crème fraîche, then adjust the seasoning to taste. Set aside.

CHEESE TOASTS

1 Preheat the grill. Mix the grated cheese with the egg and the rest of the crème fraîche. Lightly toast the bread slices, then spread the cheese mixture over one side of each slice. Dot with the rest of the butter and season with a little black pepper. Grill for 5 minutes or until bubbling and golden. Heat the soup through and serve topped with the cheese toasts.

Serves 6

Note: Little toasts covered with cheese and a dash of crème fraîche make a great topping for spinach soup, which can be made in advance and heated through before serving.

Cool Cumin-Scented Yoghurt Soup

1 teaspoon cumin seeds

1 teaspoon nigella (black onion) seeds

1 tablespoon ghee or butter

4 green onions, finely sliced

10 fresh mint leaves

2 teaspoons ground cumin

1 teaspoon turmeric

55g cashew nuts

285g canned chickpeas, drained
and rinsed

2 cups plain low-fat yoghurt

⅘ cup sour cream

⅘ cup water

600g cucumbers

1 tablespoon sugar

salt and pepper, to taste

2 tablespoons shredded coconut,
toasted

mint leaves, to garnish

1 Heat a frypan (no oil) then add the cumin seeds and nigella seeds and toss them around the hot pan until they smell roasted and seem to 'pop' around the pan (about 3 minutes). Remove the seeds and set them aside.

2 Add the ghee or butter to the pan and add the finely sliced green onions and mint leaves and sauté for a few minutes until the green onions have wilted. Add the cumin, turmeric and cashew nuts and toss until the spices are fragrant and the nuts are golden. Add the drained chickpeas and cook for a further 2 minutes. Set aside.

3 In a mixing bowl, whisk together the yoghurt, sour cream and water until smooth. Season to taste with salt and pepper. Peel the cucumbers and scrape out the seeds. Cut the cucumber flesh into thin slices and add to the yoghurt mixture.

4 Add the onion/spice mixture to the yoghurt and stir thoroughly to combine all the delicious flavours. Allow the flavours to blend for 1 hour before serving. Garnish with toasted coconut, sliced mint leaves and a few nigella seeds.

Serves 4

Note: This traditional Muslim soup is served often during the month-long Ramadan when Muslims fast from sun up to sundown and therefore need a hearty evening meal.

Curried Broccoli and Split Pea Soup with Garlic Naan

2 teaspoons corn oil

1 onion, sliced

1 tablespoon Madras curry paste

1 cup yellow split peas

½ cup brown lentils

4 cups vegetable stock

500g English spinach, washed and chopped

285g broccoli, cut into florets

1 tablespoon lemon juice

GARLIC NAAN (INDIAN BREAD)

2 plain naan or pita rounds

2 cloves garlic, crushed

1 tablespoon corn oil

1 teaspoon cumin seeds

1 Heat the oil in a large pot, add the onion and curry paste and cook for a few minutes until the onion is soft and the curry paste is fragrant.

2 Add the split peas, lentils, vegetable stock and 2 cups water and bring to the boil, skimming occasionally to remove any scum. Cover and simmer for 1 hour or until both the peas and the lentils are quite soft.

3 Add the chopped spinach and broccoli and simmer for a couple of minutes until the broccoli is tender. Season with lemon juice.

GARLIC NAAN (INDIAN BREAD)

1 To make the garlic naan: Preheat oven to 180°C. Put the naan onto 2 non-stick baking trays, brush them with the combined garlic and oil, then sprinkle with cumin seeds. Wrap in foil and bake for 15 minutes or until warmed through. Cut into thick strips and serve hot with the soup.

Serves 6

Thai Spiked Pumpkin Soup

2 tablespoons olive oil

1 large brown onion

4 cloves garlic

1 small red bird's eye chilli

½ bunch coriander

½ teaspoon chilli paste

1 teaspoon ground cumin

1 teaspoon turmeric

500g pumpkin

500g butternut squash
  (kabocha squash)

500g Japanese pumpkin

6 cups vegetable stock

400g can coconut milk

1 Heat the olive oil in a large saucepan and add the onion and garlic and cook for 10 minutes to caramelise gently. Add the chilli and coriander stems (finely chopped) and stir until fragrant.

2 Add the remaining spices and heat until toasted. Add all the pumpkin pieces and stir to coat with the spice mixture. Cover with a lid and cook over a low heat for 30 minutes until the pumpkin is beginning to soften and turn brown. Add just enough stock to cover, and stir well.

3 Simmer for 1 hour, then add the coconut milk and simmer for a further 15 minutes. Purée then serve, garnished with extra chillies and coriander.

Serves 6

Traditional French Onion Soup

8 large onions

4 tablespoons sherry or port

100g butter or oil

8 rounds of bread

2 cloves garlic, minced

½ cup grated Gruyère cheese

1½ tablespoons plain flour

½ cup grated Parmesan cheese

1 tablespoon sugar

salt and pepper, to taste

4 cups good quality vegetable stock

½ cup finely chopped parsley

2–3 cups water

½ cup red wine

1 Peel and slice the onions into rounds. Heat the butter (or oil) and sauté the garlic and onions until they are shiny and golden brown (about 15 minutes). Add the flour and stir to allow the flour to absorb the butter residue.

2 Add the sugar, beef stock, water and wine and bring to the boil, then simmer for 45 minutes. Add the sherry and simmer 5 minutes more. Add salt and pepper to taste.

3 Grill the bread until golden. Meanwhile, mix the two cheeses and parsley in a bowl. Place a large tablespoon of cheese mixture on each round of grilled bread and grill until cheese is hot and bubbling.

4 Place one round of bread in each soup bowl and then ladle boiling soup over. The crouton will rise to the top of the bowl. Serve immediately.

Serves 8

Sorrel Soup

30g butter

2 leeks, finely sliced

4 medium potatoes, diced

6 cups vegetable stock

salt and freshly ground black pepper,
  to taste

6–8 sorrel or young spinach leaves,
  shredded and mixed with 1 teaspoon
  lemon juice

1 Melt the butter in a large saucepan and cook the leeks over low heat until soft. Add the potatoes and stock and bring to the boil. Lower the heat and simmer gently for 20 minutes or until potatoes are tender. Season to taste with salt and black pepper. Add the sorrel or spinach to the soup, bring to the boil and serve.

Serves 6

Chunky Fresh Tomato Soup

4 ripe tomatoes

1 tablespoon olive oil

1 clove garlic, crushed

2 tablespoons fresh herbs (parsley, basil or combination)

pinch of sugar

2½ cups vegetable stock

salt and freshly ground pepper, to taste

1   Peel the tomatoes by holding them over a gas flame for 30 seconds, then the skins will easily slip off, or cover them with boiling water, count to 10, then plunge them into cold water and remove the skin. Cut the blossom end from the tomatoes, halve them and flip out the seeds, then chop.

2   Heat the oil and add the tomatoes, garlic and 1 tablespoon of the chopped herbs. Add a pinch of sugar and cook gently for 5 minutes, then add the stock and cook for a further 5 minutes. Taste and adjust seasoning.

3   Serve immediately, sprinkled with the remaining herbs to garnish and croutons or crostini (slim bread sticks). Or cool, place in the refrigerator and serve chilled.

Serves 6

chicken soups

Chicken Vegetable Soup with Cheese Sticks

(see photograph on page 42)

2 skinless chicken breast fillets

4 cups reduced salt chicken stock

1 tablespoon rapeseed oil

2 leeks, washed and thinly sliced

2 carrots, diced

2 sticks celery, diced

3 cloves garlic, crushed

6 cups young green leaves (watercress, rocket, sorrel, baby spinach), washed

3 tablespoons fresh pesto

cracked black pepper, to taste

CHEESE STICKS

1 sheet puff pastry, thawed

3 tablespoons reduced fat cheese, finely grated

1 Put the chicken in a pot, add just enough chicken stock to cover it and poach gently for about 10 minutes or until just cooked. Set aside to cool.

2 Heat the oil in a large pot, add the leeks and cook gently for about 2 minutes until soft. Add the carrot, celery and garlic, strain the chicken poaching stock through a fine sieve and add to the vegetables with the rest of the stock. Simmer for 10 minutes. Chop the greens finely, add them to the soup and cook for a further 10 minutes.

3 Tear the chicken breasts into fine shreds and add them to the soup. Stir in the pesto and season with plenty of cracked black pepper.

CHEESE STICKS

1 Preheat oven to 220°C. Cut the puff pastry into 2cm thick strips and place on a baking tray lined with baking parchment. Sprinkle with the cheese and bake for 20 minutes or until crisp and golden.

2 Serve the soup in wide bowls with cheese sticks.

Serves 6

Thai Chicken Soup

(see photograph opposite)

2 cups rediced salt chicken stock

2 kaffir lime or lemon myrtle leaves, optional

2 stalks fresh lemongrass or 2 teaspoons bottled lemongrass

1 bunch fresh coriander with roots

5 thin slices fresh galangal or ginger

1 skinless chicken breast fillet, cut into thin strips

2 shallots, sliced

2 fresh bird's eye chillies or pinch of sugar to taste

2 tablespoons rice wine (mirin) or sherry

juice of 1 lime

1 Place stock and lime leaves in a large saucepan. Bring to the boil.

2 Meanwhile, remove the outer layers from the lemongrass. Chop. Cut the roots from two of the coriander plants. Chop. Remove leaves from remaining coriander. Set aside.

3 Place lemongrass, coriander roots and galangal or ginger in a mortar. Bruise with a pestle. Alternatively, place ingredients in a plastic food bag. Bruise with a rolling pin.

4 Stir lemongrass mixture into stock. Bring to simmering. Simmer for 2–3 minutes. Add chicken and shallots. Simmer for 5–6 minutes or until chicken is cooked.

5 Place reserved coriander leaves, chillies, sugar, fish sauce and lime juice in a small bowl. Mix to combine.

6 To serve, divide the mixture between warm soup bowls. Ladle over the soup. Mix gently to combine. For a main meal, serve with steamed jasmine rice.

Serves 2

Thai Broth with Chicken and Vegetables

1 stalk lemongrass

1.2 litres chicken stock

4 tablespoons Thai fish sauce

1 tablespoon caster sugar

1 red chilli, deseeded and sliced

1 clove garlic, sliced

2.5cm piece fresh ginger, thinly sliced

3 skinless boneless chicken breasts,
  thinly sliced

1 carrot, cut into matchsticks

1 stick celery, sliced

4 green onions, sliced

juice of 1 lime

1 tablespoon each of roughly chopped
  fresh coriander, mint and basil

1 spring onion, shredded, to garnish

1 Peel the outer covering from the lemongrass stalk, then finely chop the lower white bulbous part and discard the fibrous top. Place the lemongrass stock, fish sauce, sugar, chilli, garlic and ginger in a saucepan. Bring to the boil, then reduce the heat and simmer, covered, for 10 minutes to release the flavours.

2 Add the chicken slices to the broth and cook for 2 minutes, then add the carrot, celery and green onions and cook for a further 5 minutes or until the vegetables and chicken are cooked and tender. Add the lime juice and herbs to the broth and heat through. Garnish with the shredded spring onion.

Serves 4

Note: While Asian soups are often served as a refreshing end to a meal, you will find this soup perfect at any time of the day or night.

Whole Chicken Soup

1½ chicken

1 leek, washed

4 slices fresh ginger

2 carrots, cut into matchsticks

1 leek, washed and sliced

2 sticks celery, cut into matchsticks

salt

2 tablespoons white wine or dry sherry

1 cup broken egg noodles or soup pasta

1 Wash the chicken inside and out and remove the neck and giblets. Place the chicken, neck and giblets into a large saucepan with enough water to cover. Add the leek and ginger. Bring to the boil and simmer, covered, for 30 minutes. Remove the leek, chicken neck and giblets. Add the carrots, leek and celery to the soup and season with salt. Add the wine and noodles.

2 Simmer a further 15 minutes until tender. Remove the chicken, cut off the joints and, if desired, cut each in two, remove the skin and return to the pan. Serve with crusty bread.

Serves 4

Note: For more formal occasions serve the soup from a soup tureen, giving each guest 2–3 pieces of chicken topped with soup.

Chicken Minestrone

olive oil spray

1 onion, finely chopped

1 clove garlic, chopped

1 stick celery, diced

1 carrot, diced

400g can peeled tomatoes

1 litre water

freshly ground black pepper

1 teaspoon dried oregano

1 teaspoon mixed spice

2 tablespoons chopped fresh parsley

85g cut macaroni

¼ cabbage, shredded

145g frozen baby peas

200g chicken breast, chopped

1 Lightly spray the base of a large saucepan with olive oil spray. Add the onion and garlic, stirring over heat until they colour a little. Add the celery and carrot and continue to stir over heat for 1 minute.

2 Chop the tomatoes and add to the saucepan with the juice. Stir in the water, pepper, oregano, spice and parsley. Bring to the boil and add the macaroni. Stir until soup returns to the boil, turn down to a simmer and cook for 15 minutes. Stir in cabbage, peas and chicken.

3 Simmer for 15–20 minutes. Serve hot with crusty bread.

Serves 4–6

Note: If the soup is too salty, add a few slices of raw potato. This will remove some of the salt, but remember to remove the potato before serving.

Colombian Chicken Coriander Soup

2 tablespoons vegetable oil

2 large onions, sliced

1 leek, washed and sliced

8 cloves garlic, chopped

2 teaspoons ground cumin

large pinch of saffron threads

2 small red chillies, minced

2 bunches fresh coriander

3 litres chicken stock

6 breasts or thighs of chicken

1kg small pink potatoes, quartered

600g carrots, sliced into rounds

2 sweet potatoes, diced

2 plantains, diced

salt and freshly ground pepper

3 ears of corn

2 avocados, diced

4 green onions, finely sliced

1 Heat the oil in a saucepan and add the onions, leek, garlic, cumin, saffron threads and minced chillies and cook for 5 minutes until the spices are fragrant and the vegetables have softened.

2 Roughly chop the coriander and set aside. Tie the remaining stalks together with string. Add the chicken stock and tied coriander stems to the onion mixture, bring to the boil and simmer for 15 minutes. Add the whole chicken pieces and continue simmering the soup for 20 minutes.

3 Remove the chicken pieces and remove the meat from the bones. Slice the chicken, returning it to the soup and discarding the bones. Remove the coriander stems from the soup and discard. Add the pink potatoes, carrots, sweet potatoes, plantains and salt and pepper to taste.

4 Simmer for 20 minutes more. Just before serving, cut the corn from the ears and add to the soup with half the chopped reserved coriander. Stir through to cook the corn. Serve the soup in deep bowls, garnished with coriander, avocado and green onions.

Serves 8

Note: This national dish of Colombia is rich both in heritage and flavour, and rural villages and towns all over this country add their own spices and herbs to give this soup individuality. Basically though, the soup is thick with chicken, vegetables and spices and is almost a meal in itself!

Ginger Chicken Wonton Soup

1 tablespoon sesame oil

1–2 teaspoons chilli paste

1 tablespoon soy sauce

2 cloves garlic, minced

60g piece fresh ginger, sliced

2 litres chicken stock

220g bamboo shoots

6 green onions, sliced diagonally

WONTONS

4 fresh shiitake mushrooms

1 teaspoon Chinese five-spice powder

125g water chestnuts, drained

3 green onions, chopped

3 sprigs fresh coriander

2 tablespoons soy sauce

1 tablespoon grated fresh ginger

1 fresh chilli, minced

1 tablespoon sesame seeds

2 skinless chicken breast fillets

1 pack wonton wrappers

1 Heat the sesame oil in a saucepan and add the chilli paste, soy sauce, garlic and ginger and sauté for 1–2 minutes. Add the stock and simmer for 15 minutes. Then add the bamboo shoots and sliced green onions and set aside.

2 To make the wontons, place all the ingredients, except the wonton wrappers, in a food processor and pulse the mixture until it is well chopped. Do not over-process.

3 To shape the wontons, separate the wonton wrappers and lay them out on a bench. Place 1 tablespoon of filling in the center of each wrapper. Working with one wrapper at a time, pick up the wrapper and moisten the edges with water. Fold the wrapper into a triangle, pinching the pastry together well to enclose the filling. Wrap the triangle around your finger, carefully pinching together the opposite corners. Shape each wonton wrapper in this way.

4 Add the wontons to the simmering soup and cook them for about 4 minutes. Serve immediately.

Serves 8

Hot and Sour Chicken Soup

600g chicken breast fillets

2 tablespoons peanut oil

4 cloves garlic, minced

2 shallots, chopped

5 stems of coriander, leaves included, chopped

30g piece fresh ginger, bruised

3 small red Thai chillies, minced

3 stalks lemongrass, finely sliced

6 kaffir lime leaves, finely shredded

2 litres chicken or vegetable stock

3 tablespoons Thai fish sauce

100g dry cellophane or glass noodles

6 spring onions, diagonally sliced

juice of 1–2 limes

handful of coriander leaves

1 Cut the chicken into 1cm-thick strips. Brush the chicken strips with 1 tablespoon of peanut oil and grill or pan fry until the chicken is golden brown and slightly charred, about 3 minutes each side. Heat the remaining tablespoon of peanut oil in a large saucepan and add the garlic, shallots, coriander leaves and stems, ginger, chillies, lemongrass and lime leaves and toss in the hot oil until fragrant, about 2 minutes.

2 Add the stock and bring to the boil. Simmer for 10 minutes, then add the grilled chicken strips and simmer for a further 10 minutes. Add the Thai fish sauce and noodles and simmer for a further 2 minutes, or until the noodles are tender. Add the sliced spring onions, lime juice and coriander leaves and serve very hot.

Serves 6

Thai Rice Soup with Chicken

½ cup rice

1 tablespoon vegetable oil

1 large clove garlic, finely chopped

1 tablespoon fresh ginger, finely grated

250g chicken thigh or breast fillets,
  trimmed and diced

white pepper, to taste

2 tablespoons fish sauce

1 small onion, finely sliced

2 tablespoons fresh coriander, chopped

2 tablespoons spring onions, chopped

GARNISH

fresh coriander leaves

red chillies, finely sliced

green onions, sliced

1   Place rice in a large saucepan with 8 cups water and bring slowly to
    the boil. Simmer gently, adding more water as necessary so that mixture
    becomes a thin porridge consistency.

2   In a wok or large frying pan, heat the oil and stir-fry the garlic and ginger.
    Add the chicken and season with pepper and fish sauce. Add the onion
    and stir-fry until chicken is cooked, about 5 minutes. Stir into the rice stock.
    Just before serving, stir in the coriander and green onions. Ladle into heated
    bowls and garnish each with a few coriander leaves, chillies and spring
    onions.

Serves 4

Velvet Chicken and Sweet Corn Soup

500g boned chicken breast

large pinch of salt

2 egg whites, beaten to froth

6 cups chicken stock

400g can creamed corn

2 tablespoon cornflour blended with
  3½ tablespoons water

2 tablespoon dry sherry

1 tablespoon light soy sauce

1 teaspoon sesame oil

thin Chinese smoked ham or bacon,
  to garnish

1 Remove fat from chicken then mince, food process or finely chop until it is almost a purée. Mix in salt well and fold in egg whites. Bring stock to the boil, add corn and return soup to the boil. Thicken with cornflour mix, stirring for about 1 minute.

2 Stir in chicken purée, sherry, soy sauce and sesame oil and simmer, stirring, for 3 minutes. Serve soup (which is popular at formal banquets) garnished with finely chopped ham or cooked bacon bits. If you can't buy Chinese ham, substitute Virginia ham.

Serves 6

Spicy Tofu, Mushroom and Udon Soup

200g firm tofu, diced

1 tablespoon reduced salt soy sauce

1 tablespoon sherry or rice wine

100g dried mushrooms, sliced or
 4 whole dried mushrooms

1 lemon myrtle or kaffir lime leaf

2–3 teaspoons olive or peanut oil

2cm piece fresh ginger, thinly sliced

2 shallots, chopped or 1 spring onion,
 sliced diagonally

6 fresh shiitake or flat mushrooms,
 thinly sliced

2 cups shredded English bok choy

500g fresh udon noodles

4 cups hot chicken stock or dashi

1 tablespoon cider vinegar

1 Place the tofu, soy sauce and sherry in a bowl. Toss to coat. Marinate for
   10 minutes.

2 Place the dried mushrooms and lemon myrtle leaf in a separate bowl. Pour
   over ½ cup boiling water. Soak for 15 minutes or until mushrooms are tender.

3 Heat the oil in a wok over a medium heat. Add the ginger, shallots and fresh
   mushrooms. Stir-fry for 1–2 minutes. Add bok choy and tofu with marinade.
   Stir-fry for 1 minute.

4 Add noodles, dried mushrooms with their soaking water, stock and vinegar.
   Bring to the boil. Remove lemon myrtle leaf and discard. Serve immediately.

Serves 4

Mulligatawny Soup

1 tablespoon vegetable oil

2 onions, chopped

1 green apple, cored, peeled and chopped

1 clove garlic, crushed

2 tablespoons lemon juice

1 tablespoon curry powder

1 teaspoon brown sugar

½ teaspoon ground cumin

¼ teaspoon ground coriander

2 tablespoons plain flour

8 cups chicken stock

500g boneless chicken breast or thigh fillets, cut into 1cm cubes

⅓ cup rice

freshly ground black pepper

1 Heat oil in a large saucepan over medium heat, add onions, apple and garlic and cook, stirring, for 5 minutes or until onions are tender. Add lemon juice, curry powder, sugar, cumin and coriander and cook over low heat, stirring, for 10 minutes or until fragrant.

2 Blend flour with a little stock and stir into curry mixture. Add chicken, rice and remaining stock to pan, bring to the boil, stirring constantly. Reduce heat, cover and simmer for 20 minutes or until chicken and rice are cooked. Season taste with black pepper.

Serves 4

Note A dash of chilli sauce and a chopped tomato are delicious additions to this soup. Serve with crusty bread rolls, naan or pita bread.

meat soups

Meatballs in Egg and Lemon Soup

(see photograph on page 60)

500g beef mince

1 medium onion, minced

¼ cup chopped fresh parsley

¼ cup short-grain rice

1 egg

salt and freshly ground black pepper

⅓ cup cornflour

1 litre beef stock

50g butter

1 egg

75ml lemon juice

1 Combine the mince, onions, parsley, rice and egg in a bowl, and mix well with your hands. Season well with salt and pepper. Using one tablespoon of mixture for each meatball, shape mixture into balls, and roll in cornflour (shaking off the excess).

2 Bring the stock and the butter to the boil in a saucepan, then reduce the heat and place the meatballs in the stock. Cover with a lid, and simmer for 45 minutes (until they are cooked). Let cool slightly. Whisk the egg and lemon juice together in a bowl, then add 100ml of warm stock to the egg and lemon juice.

3 Pour this mixture back into the saucepan and heat very gently. Season with salt and pepper before serving.

Serves 6

Stone Soup

(see photograph opposite)

1 tablespoon olive oil

1 onion, finely chopped

2 cloves garlic, crushed

200g piece smoked bacon diced

250g piece smoked ham hock

2 potatoes, diced

2 carrots, diced

2 turnips, diced

2 sticks celery, diced

2 bay leaves

1½ litres vegetable or chicken stock

2 cups shredded savoy or green cabbage

400g can red kidney beans, drained and rinsed

2 tablespoons chopped fresh parsley

salt and freshly ground black pepper

1 Heat the oil in a large saucepan over medium heat. Cook the onion and garlic until soft. Add the bacon and cook for 2 minutes. Add the ham hock, potatoes, carrots, turnips, celery, bay leaves and stock.

2 Bring to the boil, reduce heat to low and simmer covered for 40–45 minutes or until vegetables are tender. Simmer for 1 hour, as this gives the soup more flavour. Add cabbage and kidney beans and simmer for a further 5 minutes.

3 Remove ham hock or bacon bones and cut the meat into small pieces. Return meat to the saucepan, add parsley and season with salt and pepper. Serve soup with crusty bread.

Serves 4–6

Note: Another idea is to serve this soup with grilled cheese triangles. Toast the required number of bread slices, cut into triangles and top with a slice of your favourite cheese and a few fresh chopped herbs.

Chunky Lamb Soup

30g butter

500g lamb fillet, cut into 2cm cubes

1 large onion, chopped

1 tablespoon fresh parsley, chopped

2 teaspoons paprika

1 teaspoon saffron powder

1 teaspoon ground black pepper

1½ litres lamb or chicken stock

60g chickpeas, soaked overnight in
water to cover

500g tomatoes, peeled, seeded and
chopped

4 tablespoons lemon juice

60g long-grain rice

1 Melt the butter in a large saucepan over moderate heat. Add lamb cubes, onion, parsley, paprika, saffron and pepper. Cook for 5 minutes, stirring frequently. Add the stock.

2 Drain chickpeas and add them to pan with tomatoes and lemon juice. Bring to the boil, boil for 10 minutes, then cover pan and simmer mixture for 1–1¼ hours. Stir in rice. Cook for 15–20 minutes or until tender. Serve at once, in heated bowls.

Serves 4

Note: Economically, a hearty meat soup is a good choice, because usually a less tender and therefore a less expensive cut of meat is used. A meat soup generally uses less meat than other dishes and is a good choice for those trying to reduce their intake of red meat.

Broccoli and Bacon Soup

1 large onion, roughly chopped

2 cloves garlic, chopped

3 rashers bacon, derinded and cut into small pieces

1 tablespoon olive oil

3 cups hot water

3 chicken stock cubes

500g broccoli

freshly ground black pepper

1 cup low-fat milk

chives to garnish

1 Heat the oil in a large saucepan and sauté the onion and garlic for 5 minutes until clear. Pour in water and crumble in stock cubes. Bring to the boil. Add broccoli and cook for 10 minutes until broccoli is just tender.

2 Purée in a blender or food processor. If you have neither of these appliances, a sieve and a wooden spoon will do the job, as will a mouli or food mill. Return soup to saucepan. Mix in bacon and milk.

3 Cook for 5 minutes. Season with freshly ground black pepper. Serve garnished with chives.

Serves 4

Beef Pho

225g thick steak in one piece

1 packet rice noodles

2 tablespoons fish sauce

455g flat, thick, dried noodles

½ cup of bean sprouts, washed

1 brown onion, thinly sliced

3 spring onions, finely chopped

½ cup fresh coriander, torn into sprigs

½ cup Vietnamese mint leaves, chopped

1 small red chilli, seeded and sliced
  into rings

2 limes, cut into wedges

STOCK

3 litres water

1kg shin beef bones

340g gravy beef

1 large brown onion, unpeeled and
  halved

3 medium pieces fresh ginger,
  unpeeled and sliced

pinch of salt

1 cinnamon stick

6 whole cloves

6 peppercorns

6 coriander seeds

4 whole star anise

2 carrots, unpeeled and cut into chunks

1 To make stock, pour the water into a large pot, add the shin bones and gravy beef and bring to the boil. Skim off foaming scum from surface. Turn heat to medium-low, partly cover and simmer for 2 hours, skimming often. Add remaining stock ingredients.

2 Simmer for another 90 minutes and remove from heat. Drain through a fine sieve, reserving stock. Discard bones, carrots, onion and spices. When cool, skim fat from stock. Cut the gravy beef finely across the grain. Slice steak to paper thin slices and set aside. Soak the rice noodles in warm water for about 20 minutes until soft. Drain and set aside. Return stock pot to boil. Add the fish sauce then reduce heat to very low. Fill a separate large pot three-quarters full of water and bring to the boil. Add the dried noodles and bean sprouts.

3 Continue boiling until noodles are tender but not mushy. Bean sprouts should retain some crispness. Pour boiling stock into six serving bowls, add drained noodles then top equally with shin meat, raw onion rings, spring onions, and raw steak slices, and garnish with coriander and mint leaves.

Serves 4

Note: Diners may help themselves to chilli rings and lime wedges. This recipe is also good with chicken which takes less time to cook.

Beef Udon Noodle Soup

85g udon noodles

1 cup udonji, heated

55g eye fillet steak, sliced very thinly

1 tablespoon sliced spring onion greens

1 tablespoon cooked tempura batter pieces

1/2 teaspoon chopped white sesame seeds

1   Cook udon noodles in boiling water for 8 minutes, until tender. Pour hot udonji into a serving bowl. Spoon in hot cooked udon noodles. Overlap slices of beef onto the noodles, covering half the bowl. Add green onions and tempura batter pieces to the soup. Sprinkle sesame seeds over the soup and serve.

Serves 1

Country Vegetable Soup with Basil

500g dried haricot beans

1 large onion

500g green beans

500g courgette

5 medium potatoes

30g butter

2–3 rashers bacon

8–10 cups water

2 teaspoons salt

BASIL PASTE

1 cup basil leaves, finely shredded

4 cloves garlic, crushed

2 ripe tomatoes, peeled and chopped

1 tablespoon tomato paste

½ cup cheese, finely grated

3 tablespoons olive oil

1 Soak the beans overnight or for several hours. Place them in a large pan with fresh water to cover. Bring to the boil, cover and simmer for 20 minutes, then drain. Meanwhile, chop the onion finely. Trim the green beans and cut them into short lengths. Cut courgette into fairly thick slices. Peel potatoes and dice.

2 Melt the butter in a large pan and sauté the bacon and prepared vegetables, including the haricot beans, until softened, (about 5 minutes). Cover with cold water and add salt. Cover with a lid and simmer gently for 1 hour.

3 Meanwhile, make basil paste and stir into soup just before serving. Serve hot with cheese toasts or crusty bread.

BASIL PASTE

1 Combine basil leaves and garlic in a bowl. Add the tomatoes to the basil with tomato paste and cheese. Pound this mixture in a blender or food processor to make a smooth paste. Gradually beat in olive oil. Set aside to serve with soup.

Balinese Egg Noodle Soup

2 carrots

1 sweet potato

145g Chinese cabbage

8 cups vegetable stock

8 green onions (green parts only)

100g dried egg noodles

1 tablespoon sweet soy sauce

MEATBALLS

6 shallots

4cm piece fresh ginger (3 teaspoons minced)

2 cloves garlic

2 tablespoons olive oil

250g minced beef

2 teaspoons ground coriander

1 egg white

1 tablespoon cornflour

salt and pepper, to taste

GARNISH

2 onions, sliced and fried until crisp

1 red pepper, finely shredded

SOUP

1 Peel and finely chop the shallots, ginger and garlic. Heat the oil and sauté until these flavourings are softened. Remove ⅓ of this mixture and reserve for the meatballs.

2 To the remaining mixture, add the carrots and sweet potato (cut into matchsticks) and sauté for 5 minutes. Add the shredded cabbage and cook until wilted (about 4 minutes). Add the chicken/vegetable stock and the julienned greens and bring to the boil. Simmer for 10 minutes.

MEATBALLS

1 To the reserved shallot mixture, add the minced meat, coriander, egg white, cornflour, and salt and pepper to taste. Mix well and form into small balls.

2 To the simmering soup, add the meatballs and allow them to boil gently for a further 5 minutes. Add the noodles, pushing them down into the soup and simmer for a further 2 minutes or until the noodles are just tender.

3 Season with the sweet soy sauce and serve garnished with fried onions and julienne of cpepper.

Serves 6–8

seafood soups

Spanish Fish Soup with Saffron

(see photograph on page 72)

2 tablespoons olive oil

2 large carrots, finely chopped

3 leeks, well washed and finely sliced

1 red pepper, chopped

1 green pepper, chopped

1 tablespoon Spanish paprika

large pinch of saffron threads

2 cups white wine

3 cups fish stock

400g firm white fish fillets, diced

400g prawns, shelled and deveined

400g baby calamari or squid

2 tablespoons chopped fresh parsley
 to garnish

1 lemon, cut into wedges to garnish

1 Heat the olive oil in a large saucepan and add the carrots, leeks and pepper and sauté until softened (about 10 minutes). Add paprika and saffron, and continue to cook for a few minutes more.

2 Add wine and stock and bring to the boil, simmering for 15 minutes. Add fish, prawns and baby calamari or squid and simmer for a further 5 minutes. Garnish with some chopped parsley and a squeeze of lemon.

Serves 4

Spiced Fish, Tomato and Chickpea Soup

(see photograph opposite)

1 tablespoon olive oil

1 onion, chopped

1 teaspoon ground coriander

1 teaspoon ground cumin

1 teaspoon allspice

1 green chilli, finely sliced

400g can chopped tomatoes

400g can chickpeas, rinsed and
 drained

4 cups reduced salt fish stock

500g firm white fish fillets (redfish,
 bream, sea perch), cut into large
 pieces

⅓ cup couscous

thick, low-fat plain yoghurt, to serve

1 tablespoon chopped fresh parsley

1 tablespoon chopped fresh mint

Lebanese bread, to serve

1 Heat the oil in a large pot, add the onion and cook over a medium heat for 3 minutes or until the onion is soft and golden.

2 Add the spices and chilli and cook until fragrant (about 2 minutes). Stir in the tomatoes, chickpeas and fish stock and bring to the boil. Reduce the heat and simmer uncovered for 15 minutes.

3 Add the fish and cook for 5 minutes or just until the fish is tender. Remove the soup from the heat then add the couscous and cover. Set aside for 10 minutes or until the couscous is soft.

4 Serve with a dollop of yoghurt and sprinkled with parsley and mint. Accompany with wedges of Lebanese bread.

Serves 6

Seafood Soup

1 tablespoon butter

2 medium onions, chopped

2 cloves garlic, chopped

2 x 440g cans chopped tomatoes

1 cup fresh, raw seafood such as
  shrimp, fish, oysters and mussels

sprinkle of chilli powder

salt and freshly ground black pepper

fresh parsley and chives, chopped

1 Melt the butter in a large saucepan. Add the onion and garlic and cook until softened. Add the tomatoes and bring to the boil. Simmer for 5 minutes, then add the seafood and simmer for a further 5 minutes. Add the seasonings, parsley and chives. Serve in warmed bowls with crusty bread.

Serves 4

Simple Seafood Bisque

500g ripe tomatoes, peeled and chopped

2 onions, diced

5 cups cold water

1 teaspoon lemon juice

salt and freshly ground black pepper

500g white fish fillets, cut into cubes

150ml single cream

2 tablespoons finely chopped fresh dill

125g small peeled shrimp

1 In a large saucepan, combine the tomatoes, onions, water and lemon juice and season with salt and pepper. Bring to the boil, then lower the heat and simmer for 20 minutes.

2 Add the fish cubes to the soup and cook until they are just tender but not falling apart. Stir in the cream, check the seasoning and add the dill and the shrimp. To serve, reheat very gently if necessary.

Serves 4–6

Fish Soup with Aioli

3 tablespoons olive oil

1½ cups chopped onion

1 leek (white and pale green part),
   cleaned and cut into 1cm-thick rounds

1 stick celery, chopped

1 carrot, chopped

1kg meaty fish bones

1 cup dry white wine

2 cups water

zest of ½ orange

3 large sprigs thyme or ½ teaspoon
   dried thyme

3 bay leaves

1 teaspoon freshly ground black pepper

1 teaspoon fennel seeds

salt

1kg fish fillets (preferably a mixture of
   sea bass, cod, snapper and halibut),
   cut in 4cm cubes

croutons

3 tablespoons minced chives to garnish

AIOLI

1½ tablespoons coarsely chopped garlic

1 teaspoon salt, plus salt to taste

3 egg yolks

1 cup olive oil

lemon juice

1 In a large stockpot over moderate heat, heat the olive oil. Add the onion, leek celery, and carrot. Reduce the heat to low and cook gently until the vegetables are soft (about 15 minutes).

2 Add the fish bones, wine, water, orange zest, thyme, bay leaves, pepper and fennel seeds. Raise the heat to moderate and bring the mixture to the boil, skimming any residue that rises to the surface. Reduce to a simmer and cook for 35 minutes. Strain soup into a clean pot. Season with salt. Return the broth to a simmer over a moderate heat.

3 Add the fish. Add the firm fish first and more delicate fish about 2 minutes later. Cook until the fish just begins to flake (3–4 minutes in total). Remove the fish to a warm platter, using a slotted spoon. Moisten with ¼ cup broth, cover, and keep warm in a low oven.

4 To make the aioli, process the garlic, salt and yolks until smooth. With the motor of your food processor running, begin adding the oil drop by drop through the feed tube. When the mixture is thick and smooth, add the oil faster. Transfer to a bowl and season to taste with lemon juice, adding more salt if necessary. Makes 2 cups.

5 Put 1 cup of the aioli in a medium-sized bowl. Whisk in ½ cup hot broth. Whisk this mixture back into the stockpot. Cook over low heat, stirring constantly with a wooden spoon, until visibly thickened (about 3 minutes). Do not allow the soup to boil or it will curdle. Garnish with the croutons, chives and remaining aioli.

Serves 4

Seafood Noodle Soup

1½ litres chicken stock

500g fish fillets, shrimp and scallops

6 fresh shiitake mushrooms, sliced

3 baby bok choy, cut into 2.5cm slices

1½ tablespoons cornstarch

2 cups water

2 teaspoons sesame oil

155g Chinese-style dry noodles

coriander leaves to garnish

1 Bring the chicken stock to the boil in a saucepan. Add the fish, shrimp and scallops. Return to the boil. Reduce the heat to a simmer; cover and cook for about 10 minutes. Add the mushrooms and bok choy and simmer for a few more minutes.

2 Blend together the cornstarch and water until smooth. Stir the blended mixture into the bubbling broth. Return to a simmer and cook, stirring occasionally, until the broth is clear and thickened (about 2 minutes). Stir in the sesame oil. Cook the noodles in boiling water in a large saucepan for 5–6 minutes. Drain and divide among 4 serving bowls. Spoon the soup over the noodles. Garnish with a few coriander leaves.

Serves 4

Fish and Rice Soup

25g butter

1 onion, finely chopped

1 clove garlic, chopped

1½ litres fish stock

1 cup long-grain rice

200g mixed fish such as prawns, scallops, mussels and white flesh fish fillets

1 cup unsweetened natural yoghurt

2 tablespoons chopped fresh parsley

1 Melt the butter in a saucepan and sauté the onion and garlic until onion is clear. Add fish stock and bring to the boil. Add rice. Cover and cook for 7 minutes. Prepare fish as necessary, cutting fillets into cubes.

2 Add to soup and cook for 4 minutes or until rice and fish are cooked. Stir in the yoghurt. Bring to the boil but do not boil. Mix in parsley and serve.

Serves 4

Abalone Chowder

2 rashers bacon (cut into 2½cm pieces)

1 medium onion, chopped

3 teaspoons freshly crushed garlic

2 sticks celery, chopped

1 large carrot, chopped

½ teaspoon freshly chopped chilli

440g can tomato pieces

2 tablespoons tomato paste

2 bay leaves

1 heaped teaspoon thyme leaves

½ teaspoon salt

½ teaspoon black peppercorns, freshly
  ground

1 cup basic fish stock

6 cups water

500g abalone steaks, ground or finely
  chopped

2 medium potatoes, diced

2 tablespoons plain flour

2 tablespoons water

2 ice cubes

½ cup dry sherry

1 Fry bacon in a large frypan (until crisp). Pour off almost all fat, keeping a small amount. Fry onion, garlic, celery, carrot and chilli in the remaining bacon fat.

2 Cook for 3–4 minutes (until vegetables are tender). Add the tomatoes, including the juice, tomato paste, bay leaves, thyme and salt and pepper. Stir in the fish stock, water, abalone and potatoes. Bring the mixture to the boil, then reduce heat to simmer. Simmer uncovered for 40–45 minutes.

3 In a jar with a tight-fitting lid, combine the flour, water and ice cubes. Shake the jar vigorously, then pour the flour and water paste into the chowder. Add the sherry. Stir and increase the heat (until the liquid boils). Allow the mixture to boil gently (until the broth thickens slightly).

4 Taste for seasoning, and add more sherry and salt and pepper (if desired).

Serves 10

Prawn and Chicken Soup

1 tablespoon vegetable oil

1 onion, diced

1 red pepper, diced

2 cloves garlic, crushed

1 teaspoon finely chopped fresh ginger

4 cups chicken stock

125g boneless chicken thigh or breast,
fillets, sliced

20 uncooked small prawns, shelled and
deveined

125g rice noodles

125g canned bamboo shoots, drained
and sliced

5 white mushrooms, thinly sliced

¼ lettuce, shredded

2 green onions, thinly sliced

2 tablespoons finely chopped fresh
coriander

1½ tablespoons soy sauce

freshly ground black pepper

1 Heat oil in a saucepan over a medium heat, add onion and red pepper and cook, stirring, for 5 minutes or until onion is soft. Add garlic and ginger and cook for 2 minutes longer.

2 Stir in stock and bring to the boil. Add chicken, prawns, noodles, bamboo shoots and mushrooms, reduce heat and simmer for 5 minutes or until noodles are tender.

3 Stir in lettuce, green onions, coriander, soy sauce and black pepper to taste, and serve immediately.

Serves 4

Crab Soup

170g can crabmeat (or fresh, picked crabmeat)

1 egg

4 dried Chinese mushrooms

85g canned bamboo shoots

1 leek

small piece fresh ginger

1 tablespoon vegetable oil

2 tablespoons soy sauce

1 tablespoon rice wine, mirin or dry sherry

6 cups fish or chicken stock

2 teaspoons salt

freshly ground pepper

1½ tablespoons cornflour

2 tablespoons parsley, chopped

1 Drain crabmeat and break up. Beat the egg in a small bowl. Soak dried mushrooms in water for 20 minutes, discard stalks, then slice caps. Drain bamboo shoots and cut them into strips, slit the leek almost through, discarding tough green, wash carefully, then cut into strips. Grate or finely chop ginger.

2 Heat the oil in a wok or medium saucepan, add the mushrooms, leek, bamboo shoots and ginger and stir- fry for 1 minute.

3 Add the crabmeat, sprinkle with soy sauce, rice wine and pour in the heated stock or water. As soon as the liquid comes to the boil, skim off any scum. Season with salt and pepper, stir in the cornflour mixed with a little water, to thicken the soup.

4 Pour in the beaten egg and mix, stirring lightly so that the egg sets in short strands. Sprinkle with finely chopped parsley and serve.

Serves 4–6

Clam Chowder

1 kg clam meat

250g butter

6 rashers bacon, finely chopped

3 onions, finely chopped

1½ cups celery, finely chopped

1 cup plain flour

5 cups milk

3 cups fish stock

10 tablespoon parsley, freshly chopped

salt and pepper, to taste

5 cups boiled potatoes, finely diced

1 Melt butter, add the bacon, onion and celery into the pot and cook until tender (about 5 minutes).

2 Add the flour and cook for 2 minutes.

3 Add the milk, fish stock and potatoes, cover and simmer for 10 minutes.

4 Add the clam meat and cook again for 10 minutes. Season to taste.

5 Serve in a deep plate with cream and parsley.

Serves 4

Note: Extra vegetables of your choice may be added – it is a good way to use up vegetable leftovers.

Mussels with Endive and Basil Soup

30g butter

2 endives, with leaves cut loose

1 cup broth from cooking the mussels, strained

2 tablespoons double cream

15 basil leaves, chopped finely

salt and pepper

1 kg black mussels cleaned, cooked Mariniére style and removed from shell

MUSSELS MARINIÉRE STYLE

1 small onion, sliced

1 stick celery, sliced

1 clove garlic, chopped

60ml white wine

pepper, to taste

1 tablespoon butter

1 tablespoon parsley, chopped

1 Melt butter in a pot and stir-fry endives.

2 Add broth, cream and basil, mix well with a whisk until ingredients all blend in together.

3 Add mussels, heat until boiling and serve in bowls.

MUSSELS MARINIÉRE STYLE

1 Place the mussels, onion, celery, garlic and white wine in a large saucepan.

2 Cook over a medium heat until the mussels have opened. Stir frequently to ensure that the mussels cook evenly.

3 Add pepper to taste. Stir in the butter and pepper just before serving.

Serves 4

Lobster Bisque

1 small lobster, cooked

1 large carrot, peeled and diced

1 small onion, finely chopped

125g butter

¾ cup dry white wine

bouquet garni

6½ cups fish or chicken stock

⅓ – ¾ cup rice

salt, pepper and ground cayenne, to taste

½ cup cream

2 tablespoons brandy

parsley, chopped

1 Split the lobster in half, lengthwise, and remove the flesh from the shell, then set it aside. Wrap the shell in an old tea towel, crush the shell with a hammer and set aside. Sauté the carrot and onion in half the butter until softened without colouring (about 5 minutes). Add the crushed shell, sauté a further minute or so then add the wine. Boil hard until reduced by half. Add the bouquet garni, stock and the rice.

2 After about 20 minutes, when the rice is tender, remove the large pieces of shell and the bouquet garni. Purée in a food processor with the remainder of the batter, doing so in small batches. Pour through a strainer. Rinse out the food processor to remove every trace of shell and purée the strained liquid again, this time with the lobster flesh, saving a few pieces for the garnish. Reheat gently.

3 Add salt, pepper and cayenne to taste, then stir in the cream, brandy and reserved lobster pieces cut into thin slices. Serve very hot, garnished with parsley.

Serves 6

Fish Noodle Soup

500g white fish fillets

vegetable oil

90g spring onions

1 teaspoon fresh ginger, chopped,

1 teaspoon garlic, chopped or crushed

1 red pepper, seeded and chopped

4 cups fish stock or water

1 tablespoon oyster sauce

½ teaspoon ground black pepper

1 teaspoon sesame oil

1 tablespoon dry sherry

250g egg noodles, boiled

1 teaspoon sesame oil, extra

½ red pepper, seeded (extra) and
  chopped to garnish

1   Chop fish into bite-sized pieces. Heat enough vegetable oil to deep-fry fish for 2½ minutes. Remove and drain. Cut spring onions into 4cm sections, separating white parts from green.

2   Heat 3 tablespoons of oil and brown ginger and soften garlic. Add fish, bell pepper and white sections of spring onions. Stir-fry for 3 minutes then add stock or water and boil. Add green spring onion sections, oyster sauce, black pepper, oil and sherry and simmer for 1 minute, stirring.

3   Add hot, cooked, drained noodles and extra 1 teaspoon of oil. Stir through until hot. Serve immediately, garnished with chopped capsicum.

Serves 4

Mussel Soup

1⅕ cups water

1 small carrot, diced finely

60g cauliflower, divided into florets

½ red pepper, diced finely

½ onion, diced finely

1 pinch saffron

10 coriander seeds, cracked

45ml sherry vinegar

85g butter

2 tablespoons plain flour

1 kg black mussels, cooked as
  Mariniére style (see page 88)

2 tablespoons double cream

salt and pepper, to taste

1 tablespoon fresh parsley, finely
  chopped

1   In a large pot on a high heat combine water, carrot, cauliflower, pepper,
    onion, saffron and coriander seeds.

2   Bring to the boil and add the vinegar. Remove from heat and allow to cool
    down.

3   When cold, strain the vegetables from the cooking liquid.

4   In a cooking pot on a medium heat, melt the butter then add the flour. Stir
    with a wooden spoon and cook gently for 2 minutes.

5   Add the broth slowly with a whisk and cook until slightly thickened, with a
    smooth consistency.

6   Add reserved vegetables, mussels, cream and bring to the boil. Taste and
    season if necessary with salt and pepper. Add parsley just before serving.

Serves 4

Rustic Mediterranean Seafood Soup

200g calamari tubes, cleaned

285g green prawns

200g mussels

250g mixed firm white fish fillets (red mullet, sea perch, red fish)

1 tablespoon olive oil

2 cloves garlic, crushed

1 onion, finely chopped

½ cup white wine

400g can tomatoes, chopped

3 cups reduced salt fish stock

pinch saffron

2 potatoes (about 285g), peeled and cut into large cubes

1 Cut the calamari tubes into rings. Peel and devein the prawns, leaving the tails intact. Scrub the mussels and remove their hairy beards. Discard any mussels that are already open. Remove any bones from the fish and cut it into large pieces.

2 Heat the oil in a large pot. Add the garlic and onion and cook over a medium heat for 3 minutes or until the onion is golden. Add the white wine and bring to the boil. Cook over a high heat until nearly all the liquid has been absorbed.

3 Add the tomatoes, fish stock, saffron and potatoes and simmer for 15 minutes or until the potatoes are tender. Do not overcook or they will tart to break up.

4 Add all the seafood and simmer for 3–5 minutes or until tender. Serve with crusty Italian bread.

Serves 6

Thai Prawn Soup with Lemongrass

125g large green prawns

3 stalks lemongrass

4 cups reduced salt fish stock

2cm piece ginger, peeled and cut into fine strips

2 kaffir lime leaves

½ small pineapple, peeled and cored

1 tablespoon fish sauce

1 tablespoon lime juice

6 spring onions, thinly sliced on the diagonal

½ cup fresh coriander leaves

pepper, to taste

1 Peel and devein the prawns, leaving the tails intact. Reserve the shells and discard the veins. Halve the lemongrass stalks and squash the bases with the flat side of a knife.

2 Place the prawn shells in a medium pot with the stock and bring slowly to the boil. Reduce the heat and simmer gently for 10 minutes. Strain, then return to the pot and add the lemongrass, ginger and lime leaves, and return to simmering point.

3 Cut the pineapple into thin pieces and add to the stock along with the prawns, and simmer just until the prawns turn pink and tender (a few minutes, depending on their size). Add the fish sauce, lime juice, spring onions and coriander.

4 Remove the lemongrass and lime leaves, season with pepper and serve immediately.

Serves 6

Maltese Mussels

500g black mussels, cleaned

2 roasted red peppers, peeled and diced

3 garlic cloves, chopped

1 orange, juice and grated zest

½ fennel bulb, diced

½ celery stick, diced

⅗ cup white wine

⅘ cup tomato juice

salt, pepper, cayenne pepper, and paprika, to taste

2 cups chicken stock

⅔ cup olive oil

1 In a large pot on medium heat, add oil, onion, garlic, pepper, tomato, fennel, celery and cook for 10 minutes.

2 Add white wine, orange juice, zest, tomato juice, chicken stock, seasoning and cook for 20 minutes.

3 Add mussels and cook until all mussels have opened, about 8–10 minutes. Discard any mussels that do not open.

4 Serve with wood–fired bread or Grissini.

Serves 4

special soups

Spinach, Tomato and Rocket Soup

(see photograph on page 98)

2 tablespoons olive oil

2 onions, finely diced

1 bunch rocket, torn

250g fresh spinach, stemmed

2 tablespoons plain flour

1 litre vegetable stock

2 tablespoons lemon juice

1kg ripe tomatoes, diced

3 eggs

1 cup sour cream

200g baby spinach leaves

salt and freshly ground black pepper

several perfect rocket leaves to garnish

½ bunch fresh chives, chopped to garnish

1 Heat the olive oil in a large saucepan and add the onions. Cook over a high heat until golden and soft, about 5 minutes. Add the torn rocket and spinach and sauté until wilted. Sprinkle the flour over the vegetables and stir to combine. Cook for another 2 minutes, then gradually add the stock and lemon juice while stirring to incorporate.

2 Add the tomatoes and simmer for 20 minutes. Break the eggs into a bowl and whisk briefly. Remove the soup from the heat and when it stops bubbling add the eggs and stir vigorously to distribute. When the soup appears more opaque (about 3 minutes), return the soup to the heat and simmer for 5 minutes.

3 Place the sour cream in a bowl and add a ladle of soup. Mix thoroughly then return to the soup. Add the baby spinach and stir through without boiling. Season to taste with salt and pepper. Garnish with a rocket leaf or two and a sprinkle of chives and serve.

Serves 6

Note: This is one of our favourite soups. The combination of tomato and rocket makes this soup rich and complex in flavour – a perfect Sunday-night supper!

Iced Curried Fruit Soup

(see photograph opposite)

2 cooking apples, cored and roughly chopped

1 banana, chopped

125g papaya, peeled, seeded and chopped

4 spring onions, finely chopped

440g can tomato juice

1 cup chicken stock

½ teaspoon curry powder

salt and freshly ground black pepper

1 cup double cream

3 tablespoons shredded coconut

1 cooking apple, peeled and coarsely grated or chopped

cooked strips of pappadum

1 Place the apples, banana, papaya and spring onions in a food processor or blender and process until smooth. Blend in the tomato juice, stock and curry powder. Pour into a large jug or bowl, adjust the seasonings and leave to chill for several hours. Place the cream in a bowl, beat until soft peaks form, and then fold in the coconut and grated apple. Leave to chill. Serve the soup with a spoonful of cream mixture and pappadum strips.

2 To cook pappadums heat 2 cups of oil in a high-sided skillet or medium-sized saucepan, until hot. Add 1 pappadum; it will quickly puff up and become golden. Remove it from the oil immediately and drain it on a paper towel. Repeat with the remaining pappadums.

3 To microwave, place 2 pappadums directly on the carousel, cook on high power, in 2-second spurts, turning over to crisp both sides. For pappadum strips, cut the uncooked pappadums into strips of various widths and cook as above.

Serves 6

Iced Tomato and Pepper Soup

2 white onions, roughly chopped

2 large green peppers, seeded and roughly chopped

2 cucumbers, peeled, seeded and chopped

2 x 440g cans whole peeled tomatoes

3 cups canned tomato juice

½ –¾ cup lemon juice

salt and cayenne pepper

ice cubes

1 Place half the onions, peppers and cucumbers in a food processor or blender. Blend until finely chopped. Add the tomatoes and blend again. Pour the mixture into a bowl and stir in the tomato juice and lemon juice. Season with salt if required and a dash of cayenne pepper. Chill thoroughly.

2 Finely chop the remaining vegetables separately and place them in small bowls for garnish. Chill until required. Place two or three ice cubes in each soup bowl; ladle or pour the soup over. Offer the prepared garnishes separately and serve with garlic croutons.

Serves 8

Gazpacho

2 slices of stale bread (optional)

2 kg tomatoes, washed and roughly chopped

1 cucumber, peeled and chopped

1 green pepper, seeded and chopped

1 small onion, peeled and chopped

2 cloves garlic, peeled and chopped

5 tablespoons olive oil

1–2 tablespoons good wine vinegar, to taste

1 teaspoon cumin seeds or cumin powder

ice cubes to cool

1 Soak bread (if using) in a little water, and squeeze it out before using. (The bread helps to thicken the soup and give it a nice consistency).

2 Blend all vegetables and garlic in a mixer, and push through a sieve into a bowl. Use the mixer again to beat bread, oil and vinegar together. Add some of the tomatoes, the cumin seeds and salt to taste. Add a little water and mix into the bowl with the soup. Add a few ice cubes and leave to become cold. You can add more water if necessary.

Serves 6–8

Lithuanian Borscht

5 large beetroots (about 1 kg)

1 cup red wine

10 small red potatoes, unpeeled

1 teaspoon salt

50g unsalted butter

2 large Spanish onions, roughly chopped

6–7 cups rich chicken or vegetable stock

1 teaspoon salt

salt and freshly ground black pepper

3 hard-boiled eggs

½ cup sour cream

2 tablespoons chopped fresh chives

1   Peel and grate 1 beetroot and mix with the red wine in a small bowl and set aside. In a large saucepan, add all the trimmed (unpeeled) beetroots and cover with cold water. Bring to the boil and simmer over medium heat for 40 minutes or until tender. In a separate saucepan, cover the potatoes with water, add teaspoon of salt and cook just until tender. Drain and cool, then dice.

2   When the whole beetroots are soft, drain and rinse under cold water, then peel by rubbing the skin off with your fingers (you may like to wear rubber gloves here). Roughly chop all but one of the beetroots and set aside. Grate the remaining beetroot and set aside separately. Put the onions and butter in a saucepan and sweat until the onions are soft and lightly golden. Add the roughly chopped beetroots and mix well. Add the stock, teaspoon of salt and the raw grated beetroot and red wine mixture and bring to the boil. Add six of the cooked and chopped red potatoes and simmer briefly to allow the flavours to blend, then purée in a food processor or with a hand blender.

3   Add the cooked grated beetroot and salt and pepper to taste. Roughly chop the hard-boiled eggs and dice the remaining potatoes. To serve, ladle the soup into bowls and place a dollop of sour cream in the centre of each bowl of soup, then pile potato pieces, chopped egg and chives over the top. Serve hot or cold.

Serves 6

Traditional Hungarian Goulash Soup

3 tablespoons olive oil

2 medium white onions, sliced

2 tablespoons Hungarian (mild) paprika

2 cloves garlic, minced

2 teaspoons caraway seeds (optional)

1 teaspoon lemon zest

2 teaspoons fresh marjoram or
 1 teaspoon dried

500g diced beef

2 tablespoons tomato paste

7 cups beef stock

2 teaspoons brown sugar

1 teaspoon salt

1 teaspoon pepper

600g potatoes, diced

1 tablespoon cornflour, mixed with
 2 tablespoons cold water

¼ cup sour cream

2 pickled cucumbers, finely diced

3 frankfurters, finely sliced (optional)

1 Heat the olive oil in a saucepan and sauté the onion until golden brown, about 5 minutes. Add the paprika, garlic, caraway seeds, lemon zest and marjoram and cook for 1–2 minutes until the mixture is fragrant. Add the beef and tomato paste, and cook until the meat is well coated and is a rich brown colour, about 5 minutes.

2 Add the stock, sugar, salt and pepper and bring to the boil. Simmer for 1 hour. Add the potatoes and continue cooking for a further 30 minutes. Check seasonings and adjust if necessary. Stir the cornflour into the soup, mixing well. Allow the soup to thicken for a couple of minutes, then serve in individual bowls.

3 Garnish with sour cream and cucumbers and frankfurters if using.

Serves 8

Note: This very thick soup is almost a meal in itself. It is flavoured with paprika, the most common spice in Hungary, and should be garnished with sour cream, finely diced pickled cucumbers and finely sliced frankfurters.

Dutch Country Cheese Soup

2 tablespoons butter

1 tablespoon olive oil

1 large onion, chopped

4 sticks celery, sliced

1kg white potatoes, peeled and diced

1 small head of cauliflower, trimmed
  and cut into florets

400g carrots, peeled and chopped

7–8 cups vegetable stock

salt and freshly ground black pepper

400g Gouda cheese, grated

6 slices country-style loaf or baguette

2 tablespoons chopped fresh chervil or
  parsley

1 Melt the butter and oil in a large saucepan until foaming. Add the onion and celery and sauté for 5 minutes until the golden. Add the potatoes, cauliflower and carrots and continue to sauté for 5 minutes until golden. Add the stock and bring the soup to the boil. Simmer for 30 minutes until all the vegetables are tender. Season to taste with salt and pepper.

2 Add 200g of the Gouda and stir gently to distribute. Grill the bread slices on both sides then top with remaining grated cheese. Grill until the cheese melts. Ladle the soup into deep bowls then top with a hot slice of the grilled cheese bread. Sprinkle with the chervil or parsley and serve immediately.

Serves 6

Note: While the idea of a cheese soup may sound unfamiliar, this soup will make a welcome addition to your recipe collection. The soup is rich, full of chunky ingredients and is very tasty.

Classic Bouillabaisse

(see photograph opposite)

STOCK

3 kg fish heads and bones

4 tablespoons olive oil

3 cups dry white wine

2 leeks, washed and sliced

2 onions, peeled and sliced

3 sticks celery

6 tomatoes, chopped

1 teaspoon peppercorns

1 bunch thyme, parsley, dill, tied
together, rinsed

4 fresh bay leaves

12 cups of water

SOUP

2 tablespoons olive oil

2 large leeks

1 large fennel bulb, finely sliced

6 shallots, peeled and sliced

3 medium potatoes, peeled and diced

large pinch of saffron threads

2 x 400g cans Italian style tomatoes

2 kg assorted fish fillets, diced

600g large prawns, peeled

1 kg mussels, scrubbed and rinsed

500g small squid, cleaned

½ bunch parsley, chopped

1 loaf sourdough bread

salt and pepper, to taste

ROUILLE

½ cup breadcrumbs

¼ cup liquid from the soup

2 large red peppers

2 small, red chillies

3 cloves garlic

1 teaspoon red wine vinegar

salt and pepper, to taste

STOCK

1 Rinse the heads and bones and set aside. Heat the olive oil in a deep saucepan, then add the fish heads and bones. Cook the fish over a high heat, stirring constantly, until the fish pieces begin to break down, scraping up anything that sticks to the bottom of the pan (about 20 minutes). Add the wine and simmer, stirring well.

1 Add the prepared vegetables, herbs, bay leaves and water and simmer for 30 minutes, skimming any scum off the surface as it appears. After 30 minutes, strain the stock thoroughly, pressing on the solids to extract as much liquid as possible. Return to the heat for a further 20 minutes, then add salt and pepper to taste. Set aside.

SOUP

1 Heat the olive oil and add the sliced leeks, fennel, shallots, potatoes and saffron and cook over a medium heat until all the vegetables are golden and soft (about 20 minutes). Add the squashed canned tomatoes and reserved fish stock and bring the soup to the boil. Add salt and pepper to taste.

2 Add the fish, prawns and mussels and simmer for 10 minutes. Add the cleaned squid and parsley and stir gently. Remove the soup from the heat and cover. Allow to rest for 10 minutes. Meanwhile, brush the sliced sourdough bread with olive oil and grill until golden on both sides. Rub a clove of garlic over each golden slice. To serve, place a slice of grilled bread on the bottom of each soup bowl and ladle the hot soup over the top, making sure that everyone gets some mussels, prawns and squid. Add a spoonful of rouille if desired.-

ROUILLE

1 First, cut the sides off the peppers and roast the peppers slices by placing them, skin side up, under a hot grill until blistered. Place the pepper pieces in a plastic bag until cool then peel and discard the skin. Chop all the ingredients in a food processor, taking care not to over process. When the ingredients are well mixed add enough olive oil and salt and pepper to taste to make a flavoursome paste.

Serves 4

Note: This soup is traditionally garnished with a rouille, a type of paste made from red capsicums and a hint of chilli.

index